Anonymous

Agents' Manual of the International Life Insurance and Trust Company

Anonymous

Agents' Manual of the International Life Insurance and Trust Company

ISBN/EAN: 9783337373405

Printed in Europe, USA, Canada, Australia, Japan

Cover: Foto ©Suzi / pixelio.de

More available books at **www.hansebooks.com**

NTS' MANUAL

OF THE

TERNATIONAL

ɑɾɑnɕɛ ɑnd 𝕿ɾust

PANY.

OFFICES:

COR. OF WASHINGTON AND MONTGOMERY STS.,

JERSEY CITY, N. J.

1869.

D. APPLETON & Co., Stationers, 90, 92 and 94 Grand Street, New York.

THE INTERNATIONAL

LIFE INSURANCE AND TRUST COMPANY,

Corner Washington and Montgomery Streets, Jersey City, N. J.

OFFICERS AND DIRECTORS.

A. O. ZABRISKIE..............Chancellor of State of New Jersey.

HENRY S. TERBELL ....of H. S. Terbell & Co., New York.

JAMES A. WILLIAMSON......of James Bishop & Co., New York.

DANIEL S. APPLETON........of D. Appleton & Co., New York.

BLAKELEY WILSON..........Pres. 2d National Bank, Jersey City.

D. JACKSON STEWARD.......150 Fifth Avenue, New York.

HOSEA F. CLARK.... ....Pres. of Common Council, Jersey City.

E. A. HAYT...................of E. A. Hayt & Co., New York.

NELSON DUNHAM............Treasurer of Savings Institution, New
Brunswick, New Jersey.

E. A. HAYT, *President.*

JAMES A. WILLIAMSON, *Vice-President.*

CHARLES D. DESHLER, *Secretary.*

JAMES C. MIX, *Superintendent of Agencies.*

M. A. MILLER, M. D., *Medical Examiner.*

PART I.

ADVICE TO AGENTS.

TO THE AGENTS

OF

THE INTERNATIONAL

Life Insurance and Trust Company.

THE diffusion of knowledge relative to life insurance, among the people, the correction of errors that may prevail among them regarding it, and the dissemination of more correct views upon a subject of such great importance, are cardinal objects which every sound Life Insurance Company has earnestly at heart, and toward which it directs a great expenditure of effort.

These important ends are sought to be attained mainly through the instrumentality of live, intelligent, and enterprising AGENTS, and by their intercourse with and personal appeals and representations to the people of the territory to which they are assigned. It is the agent who is to kindle the spark and feed the flame of knowledge respecting the operation and *rationale* of Life Insurance. Upon him nearly every thing depends. If he be lazy, or listless, or incompetent, nothing will be accomplished; while, on the other hand, if he be active, ingenious, and indefatigable, there is no limit to the results he can control. If the agents of a company are of the former class—spiritless and inefficient—it will drag its slow length along, requiring years to effect what ought to have been accomplished in months. But if they are like the latter—wide awake, spirited, and efficient

—its business can be rapidly extended, almost indefinitely, to the public benefit and their own advantage.

It is, therefore, of the first importance to every *bona fide* and well-regulated Life Insurance Company, that its Agents be thoroughly posted and well trained in the *working details* of their profession; that they be good judges of men, and of the best modes of influencing human action. Many of the Agents of THE INTERNATIONAL LIFE INSURANCE AND TRUST COMPANY are fully up to this standard, and need little further assistance. What they know is the fruit of long practice and a wide experience. The practical suggestions, therefore, which follow, are not intended for them; but it is characteristic of their class and kind that they are ever ready to appropriate and profit by the judgment and experience of others. An accomplished Agent is ever eager to learn, and is always learning. He neither asks nor cares who is his teacher: whether he be a novice or an expert is all one to him, so long as he knows something that is worth knowing. To use the language of an old proverb — "All are fish that come to his net." There are, however, numbers among those who are honorably exerting themselves in the cause of Life Insurance, as Agents of this Company, who are desirous of rapidly acquiring the greatest attainable proficiency in their calling. To these we specially dedicate what follows, and express the hope that it may prove of substantial service to them in extending the sphere of their influence and in advancing our conjoint interests.

What constitutes a Good Agent?

He must have Faith in his Company.

No Life Insurance Agent can expect to be successful in the prosecution of his business, unless he has complete confidence in the *responsibility of the Company* which he represents, and is thoroughly persuaded of the *benefits and advantages attending the practice of Life Insurance.* If he has not this faith in his Company, he cannot impart it to those whom he seeks to insure.

But if he is able, conscientiously and unreservedly, to commend his Company, he will cause those whom he addresses to reflect his own feelings and to share his confidence. So again, if he is not convinced in his own mind of the great benefits which Life Insurance secures, he cannot reasonably expect to impress its advantages upon others. He must first *believe* in it himself, in order to make those whom he would influence believe in it also.

THE INTERNATIONAL LIFE INSURANCE AND TRUST COMPANY therefore invites and urges those who are acting as its agents to make the fullest and most searching inquiries as to the responsibility of the Company, the standing of its officers and directors, and the wisdom and security of its various plans. If there is the shadow of a doubt, let it be cleared away, so that your action may be free and unimpeded by it. Full responses will be cheerfully made to any such inquiries if addressed to the Home Office.

He must give his Time.

It is essential that an Agent should give the *necessary time and attention to the business.* To use a common saying, he must have life insurance "on the brain." Whenever he sees a man, his first thought should be, "Is he insured? Cannot I insure him?" And he must at once act practically upon the thought, by choosing an early and favorable opportunity to present the claims and merits of his Company to the party. As to this "favorable opportunity" of which we speak, a good Agent will be able to do much to create his own opportunity—by proper introductions, or by a due exercise of tact and discretion.

He must work for one Company only.

As his business will demand and amply compensate him for devoting to it all his time, so he must not fritter away his opportunities by a *divided allegiance.* He must act for *one Company only* if he would act efficiently. Either the results which he accomplishes, being distributed among two Companies, will make him of little value to the one or the other ; or, he cannot present the claims of either with any measure of earnestness if his preferences and exertions are divided between two Companies. He will infuse his own hesitation and irresolution upon those he canvasses, and will get comparatively nothing for his pains.

He must have Faith in Himself.

While an Agent must have faith in his Company and in the principle of Life Insurance if he would achieve success, so he *must also have faith in himself* if he would impress other men favorably. To this end he should cultivate energy and decision of character, strength of purpose, and quickness of perception. For his principal business will be to persuade to his way of thinking those who are *wavering* and *undecided.* He must incline the balance by the exhibition of a stronger will than theirs. If he be timid, feeble, and irresolute himself, he will never convert others to decisiveness and resolution. He will be fully as apt to *receive* as to *give* impressions ; whereas the secret of his trade is to *make* impressions which will influence action.

But do not let us be misunderstood. Loudness of speech, the "gift of gab," and an impetuous and boisterous mode of expression, are far from being tokens of a resolute spirit and strong will. Most commonly, great weakness and shallowness are, the rather, betokened thereby. A man of iron will and invincible energy may also be—nay, he usually is—quiet and unassuming in his demeanor. Under an affable and gentle bearing, therefore, cultivate steadiness of purpose, an inflexible resolution, and a will that never tires or gives up. Acquire these essentials, and then, if you *master* the details of your business, you will come across few men whom you may not *master* also, to the extent that you need. And if to this you add a conscientious conviction that men will be materially benefited, their families blessed, and society ameliorated by the beneficent business of which you are the advocate, you need not fear to look any man squarely in the face, and courteously to challenge his attention and scrutiny.

He must not be easily discouraged.

An Agent *must not be easily discouraged.* He must be patient under disappointment. He must train himself—as Mark Tapley did—to become *jolly* under discomfitures. If his overtures are declined at one time—as undoubtedly they will be again and again—he must make up his mind to try again, and console himself by the hope that he will have "better luck next time." Men's moods and temperaments vary at different times; and it often happens that a refusal, made in a moment of indifference or irritation, if received with imperturbable good-nature, is succeeded by a successful result, under a changed frame of mind and more favoring circumstances.

He must post Himself as to his People.

An Agent will find it greatly to his advantage to *inform himself thoroughly as to the circumstances* of those among whom he labors. He should systematically ascertain and make a note of, for future use, all that he can discover upon the following points, each of which will suggest persuasive arguments to an ingenious Agent :

Who of my neighbors are uninsured ? If this inquiry be prosecuted thoroughly, an Agent will be greatly surprised to find how large a proportion of his neighbors and townsmen are still not insured, presenting a most inviting field for effort.

Is such a one unmarried ? If unmarried, has he an aged parent, or young brother or sister, who is in dependent circumstances ?

Is he engaged to be married ?

If married, how recently ? If not recently, has he children, and how many ?

If a widower, has he a family of children whose circumstances will be straitened if he should die ?

If married to a second wife, has he children by the first mar-

riage for whom he may be solicitous to make a special provision?

Is he engaged in a business which, though *now* successful, is
of such a nature as to be liable to depreciation or reverses?

Is his property encumbered by a mortgage which might be
paid off at his death by a life policy?

Is he already insured; and if so, for what amount? Is it
for less than he can afford? Cannot he be prevailed upon to
duplicate it, to the extent of his ability?

These, and many other systematic inquiries, which will suggest themselves by experience, should be carefully made and
promptly acted upon.

Get Applications the Best Way to learn.

The first step toward approving one's self a good and successful Agent is *to learn how to get applications.* Very little time
need be wasted by an Agent in acquiring a knowledge of the
whole science of Life Insurance. That would be a long and
difficult task. All that is essential is an intelligent comprehen-
sion of the general principles of the business, so as simply to
enable the Agent to respond to the questions naturally arising in
the mind of a person as to the merits of the different plans offered by
all responsible Companies. If an Agent is wise, he will expend
very little preliminary effort in studying up the theory of the *science*,
but will apply himself without delay and with all his powers of
persuasion, ingenuity, and influence of every kind, to the *practical work* of getting applications. One application is the seed
of another. It will encourage the Agent himself, by the success
it marks, and the pecuniary advantages it brings; and it will
influence others by its example. We reiterate again and again
to our Agents, "Get applications." Give all your exertions to
this end. As Demosthenes alleged that the great secret of
oratory was comprised in the words, "action, action, action;"
so successful Agents, everywhere, agree that the great secret of
their success is to be found in the words, "applications, applications, applications."

He must insure Himself.

If an Agent would have others insure their lives, he must first insure his own. Failing to do this, he will often be non-plussed by the question, "Are you insured in this Company?" If he is forced by the facts of the case to reply "No," he will find it extremely difficult to persuade others to do what he has himself declined to do. Men will doubt his earnestness when he presents to them the advantages of Life Insurance if he is himself uninsured ; nor can he expect to prevail upon them to have faith in his company when he has failed to exhibit it himself.

He must not confine Himself to Friends.

It is a mistaken idea under which some Agents labor, that they cannot succeed and must not apply outside of the circle of their immediate friends and acquaintances. It is natural and right, and will unquestionably prove advantageous, to appeal to one's friends, without overlooking one of them. But many of the most successful Agents prefer to operate among entire strangers. Our advice would be that, not overlooking his friends, an Agent should canvass every person in a street, ward, or city, as systematically and exhaustively as if he were compiling a directory; calling upon and striving to persuade every man—the mechanic, the merchant, the professional man, the clerk, and others—who is at all likely or able to insure ; only omitting to call upon those whom he *knows* will not or cannot insure, or deferring to another occasion such as would absorb time that may be employed to greater immediate advantage in another direction.

He must extend his Acquaintances.

Agents will derive material assistance from notes of introduction to particular parties from their own personal friends and those whom they themselves insure. By the expenditure of some effort and influence, an Agent may secure introductions to every person that he thinks open to insurance; and thus he will be enabled to extend his circle of acquaintances almost indefinitely, and be saved the awkwardness natural to persons who are complete strangers to each other.

When an Agent has succeeded in getting an application, it will be found to be an excellent mode of introduction to a new subject, and to afford a favorable opportunity for another solicitation, if he will prevail upon the party making the application, when answering question twenty-six of the printed form, to refer to some particular friend who is not insured, or who he thinks may be influenced by his example. Upon taking the application to the friend for his certificate, an excellent opportunity will be afforded to urge him to " go and do likewise."

Another effective method of extending your business acquaintance is to prevail upon your own intimate friends, and those with whom you may have become familiar from having insured them, to give you lists of persons with whom they are on terms of special intimacy, and to whom they are willing you shall plead their example and the weight of their recommendations and influence.

Personal Solicitation all-important.

Agents should ever bear in mind that nothing can be effected without direct personal solicitation. A note—no matter how eloquently worded or strongly indorsed—will not bring a man to give you an application; and an advertisement, however lengthy, will prove equally abortive. Nothing will be effective but the magnetism of personal contact; combined with the tact and persuasiveness with which you present your claims to their sympathy, and display the merits of your Company and the advantages of Life Insurance. Go, then, in person. Go when the party is at leisure. Go when he is alone. Be cautious not to be drawn into antagonism with him. Strive to make a favorable impression; for if a man contracts an aversion to the Agent, no Company can present sufficient attractions, and no business advantages large enough to counterbalance his dislike. All this is not inconsistent with the most thorough manliness and the most laudable pride. There need be no insincerity, nor hypocrisy, nor sycophancy ; but merely a judicious observance of times and seasons, of courtesy and tact, in fine, of *plain common-sense.*

The Procrastination Excuse.

A great obstacle in the way of a Life Insurance Agent is the tendency of people to procrastinate—to put off till to-morrow, or next week, or some other " more convenient season " — that which can and ought to be done to-day.

If an Agent yields to this tendency, he will never accomplish any thing. But he will find that, by the exercise of a discreet persistency, in a majority of instances, the excuse can be surmounted. Persons who are *undecided* naturally incline to procrastinate. They " put off " merely as a pretext, and because it is easier to do so than to come to a decision. And if an Agent is a man of discrimination and resolution, he will ask no more favorable subject to operate upon than a person who is *irresolute* and *undecided.* A man who has obstinately made up his mind that he will not insure, is an unpromising, though far from a hopeless subject. But one whose mind is *not* made up, who is undecided, who is wavering, *is half won already.* He is trembling in the balance, and only a slight amount of address and energy will be required to turn the scale as the Agent wishes. It is the observation of an experienced and successful solicitor that, as soon as he finds a party undecided and irresolute, he never leaves him till he has his application in his pocket.

Not only the person solicited but the Agent himself has this same proneness to put off to another day what ought to be done *now.* An Agent is very apt to compromise with his convenience, or his inclination, by acting upon the idea that another time will suffice as well as the present for calling upon a party whom he has in view. But, in the mean time, another and more enterprising Agent may have carried off the prize. An Agent is also apt, after having nearly brought a person up to the sticking-point, to suffer some trivial difficulty, or a feeling of fatigue, or a sense of security, to intervene and postpone the completion of the all-important application to another day. But *another day* may make the man of *another mind :* he may have been seduced away by a competing Agent ; or he may have become cold and impracticable ; and all the past has been labor lost, or the ground will all have to be gone over again. The only true rule for the wide-awake Life Insurance Agent to act upon is to leave no work unfinished which can possibly be completed ; to " strike while the iron is hot;" and *never to trust any other time than the present.*

About Occasional Effort.

Occasional effort in the work of Life Insurance can never command greatly successful results, any more than it can in the prosecution of any other business. To be rewarded by success, an Agent must put forth constant, unwearied, and systematic effort. Without labor there have never been any grand achievements ; but by it all things may be overcome. This labor, then, is the price which an Agent must pay for the realization of great results ; and he will act wisely if he do not higgle about the terms.

If an Agent will reflect that there is no other business by which such large pecuniary rewards can be secured *without the outlay of any capital,* as there may be by Life Insurance, he will perceive that it is to his immediate interest to devote to his work all the time and effort that it may require. He will be amply repaid for the expenditure. Every thing depends upon himself. If he works spasmodically, fitfully, and feebly, or if he is timid and irresolute in his mode of presenting his company to the notice of the public, he cannot expect and he will not merit success. But if he is vigorous, persistent, zealous, and enterprising, these qualities will bring their own reward, in Life Insurance as in every other walk of life.

Insurers must be sought.

Agents should bear constantly in mind that men will not present themselves of their own accord to be insured. In almost every other business it is different from this. The buyer usually presents himself and asks for the commodity he needs. In Life Insurance the process is inverted. It must be carried to men. They must be called upon and their attention fastened upon it, even against their will. They must be made acquainted with the details of its operation, and its benefits must be made clear to them. They will not call upon the Agent and beg to be enlightened on these points, for, unfortunately, men generally are careless and indifferent regarding them. The information must be taken to them and the inducements made so apparent, that continued indifference makes them chargeable with folly, and even with criminal neglect.

Antagonism not to be provoked.

Be careful not to excite the antagonism of the party you are trying to influence. And, that this may be avoided, never allow yourself to be drawn into a heated discussion with him. *Oppose* as little as possible what he may advance. Either concede or evade his objections, if urged with vehemence; and, by a skilful flank movement, bring up such points as he regards with more favor. An example, taken from actual experience, will best illustrate this advice: An agent called upon a successful merchant who prided himself upon his knowledge of finance, in order to solicit an application from him. The Endowment plan of Insurance was the strong point of this Agent; and as a rule he urged, and was able to influence, persons to insure in this mode in preference to any other. But very early in his interview with the party in question, that gentleman commenced a strong denunciation of the Endowment plan of Insurance on grounds of mere financial policy, and showed that for some reason he was especially irritable on the subject. The Agent wisely avoided being drawn into antagonism to him, though convinced that his arguments were untenable and might be rebutted. "But," said the Agent to himself, "I am not here to dispute or to argue with this man, but to insure him." So, admitting to the gentleman that there was great force in his objections, he brought the Ten-Payment Life plan to his notice as not being open to the faults that he perceived in the Endowment plan. Very soon the gentleman became interested, then favorably impressed, and finally an application was secured from him. Afterward it transpired that, a few days before, the gentleman had been involved in a discussion with a less judicious Agent, who had striven to force him to his views in favor of an Endowment policy, and they had parted mutually angry. This example carries its own lesson to Agents.

Avoid Disputes with other Agents.

An Agent should never suffer himself to be beguiled into controversies with other Agents, as to the demerits of their several Companies. Not only will bad feeling be engendered, if that error is fallen into, but valuable time will be lost which might have been devoted to a successful effort to procure an application. Moreover, those who witness such controversies, and who listen to the attempts on each side to depreciate the other, will be apt to think that neither is to be trusted.

Again : Agents should never attack another Company. Whatever they may say against them may be turned against the general interest which all Life Insurance Companies have in common ; and thus the Agent, or the Company which he represents, or the beneficent system of which he is the advocate, may be brought into disrepute or disfavor. As a general fact, Life Insurance Companies are worthy of public confidence, and an injury is done to all of them by an attack upon the reputation of any one of their number.

Try for Large Policies.

As a general rule, try to get large policies. Not that small policies are undesirable, for the contrary is the fact; and an earnest believer in Life Insurance—which every Agent should be, or he has mistaken his vocation—will desire to spread its benefits among all classes, especially among the poor. But, as a matter of fact, a large policy from a prominent and wealthy man exerts a powerful influence, by the force of example, upon those who are less popular or wealthy. Besides, it requires no more time nor effort, no greater outlay of argument and persuasion, to secure a policy for $10,000 than it does to secure one for $1,000; while your own profit, as you are well aware, will be in proportion to the premium that is paid.

Numerous Competitors no Injury.

Be not discouraged if you find a great number of other Companies represented by other Agents, all of whom are diligently cultivating the same field as that to which you are assigned. The more thoroughly a field is worked the greater will be the crop; and, if you are wide awake, industrious, and expert at your occupation, you will often reap the fruits of seed that others have sown. Besides, in districts that are well worked, your labor will be lighter in proportion as the people are enlightened upon Life Insurance and understand its benefits. Where the ground is new and untilled, an immense amount of work is necessary to bring the public up to the requisite standard of knowledge. Where it is best understood, its merits will be generally recognized and the popular mind favorably prepared for it.

Practical Suggestions.

Never persist in presenting your claims upon a business man when he is preoccupied or engaged. A person thus interrupted will always be irritable, and prone to dismiss you with an abrupt and peremptory refusal. Wait for a more favorable time, and your tact and delicacy will be rewarded by a patient hearing.

Never attempt to persuade a person to insure with you in the presence of a third party. If you do, you will have two to one to contend against. Try and secure an interview when you can have him all to yourself and have his undivided attention.

Do not lower your profession by becoming a bore and a nuisance, nor by exaggeration and falsehood. Promise nothing but what can be performed. Convince those whom you canvass that, while you are obliged by a patient hearing, and esteem it a great favor to be allowed to unfold your business, they are themselves a party interested. Be modest in your demeanor, but yet show that you believe in and are not ashamed of your business.

Try to get the party you are addressing to indicate a preference for some one of the plans you have to present over another. Defer to his expressed preference, if it be decided. Find out his age. Show him how little a policy would cost. When he begins to manifest an interest, exhibit an application, and lead him to assist you to commence filling it out. Thus, you will gradually exchange action for indecision, and induce him to commit himself to the contract implied in the application.

Call on young men who are about to be married, and show them how graceful and appropriate an act it would be, and what an evidence of their confidence and affection, to take out a policy for the benefit of a betrothed.

Call on young persons who have just been married; and, while their affections are warm and lively, urge them to insure for the benefit of their young brides.

Call upon all young men, whether married or single, and demonstrate to them how cheaply insurance can be effected, and the advantages that will flow from it.

Ascertain the birthdays of your acquaintances, and induce parents to make a birthday present of a life policy to their sons. So also of sons to their parents, or one brother to another.

Get invited to call again.

If it is clear to your judgment that a party cannot be induced to give you an application at present, be cautious not to make the blunder of forcing him into a rejection of your suit. Better let him remain irresolute and undecided, and therefore still open to conviction. There is always hope so long as he does not give you a peremptory " no." By the exercise of tact and adroitness you can lead him to give you a general invitation to call again, or, better still, to *fix a time* for you to call. If you can manage to get him to accede to such an *appointment*, a great point will have been gained, and your way materially smoothed.

Concentrate Attention.

When you are trying to persuade a man to give you a policy, do not think it necessary to teach him the *whole science* of Life Insurance. Be careful not to overdo the matter by undue loquacity, or seek to " talk him down." You will weary him to death if you act upon that plan, and will inevitably disgust him with yourself, with your Company, with Life Insurance, and with all that appertains to it. He will recall the words of an old poet—

> "She told me I should surely never perish
> By famine, poison, or the enemy's sword;
> The hectic fever, cough, or pleurisy,
> Should never hurt me, nor the tardy gout;
> But, in my time, I should be once surprised
> By a strong, tedious talker, that should vex
> And almost bring me to consumption,"

and he will flee from you as he would from famine or a pestilence.

Contrary to this, *study to be as concise and as little of a bore as possible.* Strive to *concentrate*, not to *disperse* and *distract*, your own efforts and the attention of the person you seek to insure. Exert your ingenuity to ascertain his surroundings, and what mode of insurance is best adapted to them. Fix his thoughts on those merits and advantages of insurance which are peculiarly suitable to his case. Select some *one* of the plans you have to offer—for instance, the Ten-Payment Plan—and concentrate his attention, almost exclusively, upon it and its benefits. Show its superiority over the other plans—without depreciating them, however—in the points of its comparative cheapness, the brevity of its period of payments, the security it affords against forfeiture, and its profitableness as an investment. In a large majority of cases, as experience has shown, the interest of the party solicited will be enlisted by these means, and he will take the kind of policy which the Agent had previously made up his mind to procure. If, on the other hand, an Agent has no choice of his own, and no definite plan to propose, but *wanders* himself, and causes the person he would influence to *wander*, over all the various plans that may be suggested, the end will be that he will only create " confusion worse confounded " in the mind of his hearer, and produce a profound weariness and distaste for every thing that bears the most remote relation to Life Insurance.

Arguments and Inducements.

It is natural that Agents should wish to be amply fortified with persuasive arguments and inviting inducements, by means of which they may the more easily influence applications. And, to meet this want, some Companies and Agents have been misled into the adoption of a policy which ultimately reacts to the disadvantage of themselves and the public. *Companies* have been induced to propose *new* and *untried* kinds of Insurance, which either have not been tested by experience or have been condemned by it; *Agents* have been beguiled into making *promises* which it has been impossible to fulfil ; and the *public*, smarting under the non-fulfilment of expectations they had been led to entertain, have contracted a distrust of Life Insurance generally, and refuse to avail of its benefits. Aside from the immorality of such a course, it is *unnecessary* and *impolitic*. Legitimate Life Insurance affords solid and unquestionable advantages, in sufficient abundance to satisfy all reasonable demands ; and any attempt to supplement these by visionary or impracticable schemes can result only in disappointment on the one hand and disaster on the other.

Avoiding all such schemes, THE INTERNATIONAL LIFE INSURANCE AND TRUST COMPANY, while it will write every approved kind of policy which has stood the test of experience, and is written by other sound Companies, rejects all plans that are *doubtful* and *untried.* Its motto is, ECONOMY, SECURITY, STABILITY, and a PERMANENT FULFILMENT OF ALL ITS ENGAGEMENTS. It therefore would impress upon its Agents the policy of presenting the *conservatism* of this Company as a strong inducement for insuring with it; and urges them in all their representations to have the strictest regard to truth. Especially should they steer clear of the error of promising that which cannot be performed.

For the guidance of Agents, attention is invited to the following recapitulation of the advantages this Company offers—some of which are peculiar to it:

1. The International Life Insurance and Trust Company is conducted upon the mutual plan, by which policy-holders are entitled to a participation in the profits.

2. Its policies are secured against forfeiture by their specific terms.

3. It offers especial advantages to the young by equitably proportioning their premiums to their age. In most other Companies, persons *under* 25 are charged the same premium as those who have attained that age; and in nearly all the remaining Companies those who are *under* 20 pay the same as those at 20. On the other hand, this Company charges all persons, from 15 to 24 inclusive, *pro rata*, according to their age. Thus a person of 15 pays $15.66 per year, a person of 16 pays $15.85 per year, a person of 17 pays $16.16 per year, a person of 18 pays $16.49, and a person of 19 pays $16.83 per year, to insure $1,000; while other Companies charge all these ages one common rate, varying from $17.00 to $19.89 per year, for $1,000 of insurance. This feature is peculiarly worthy of the attention of Agents. And in this connection the fact is worthy of observation, that young persons from 15 to 23 have been *systematically overlooked* by the body of solicitors, and afford an inviting field for effort.

4. The business of the Company is conducted with a rigid re-

gard to *economy*. It allows only moderate salaries and commissions, respectively, to its Officers and Agents. This is a strong
argument, of which an acute Agent will not be slow to avail himself. None know better than experienced Agents that the *weak
spot* of Life Insurance, in the estimation of the public, is the expense involved in the high rate of commissions allowed by some
Companies to Agents. The public feel that this is so much ab-
stracted from the policy-holder, nor can they be made to understand how it can be legitimately afforded. And this reacts upon
the Agent. Each one of our Agents is aware—from his own experience—that our Company is not open to this objection; and
he can convert the fact into an argument to prevail on the public
to insure with us.

5. This Company does not charge the policy-holder any fee
for the policy or for the revenue stamp accompanying it.

6. It has a chartered capital of $500,000, of which $200,000
is paid up ; and it deposits with the State Treasurer $100,000 as
a perpetual guarantee for the security of policy-holders.

7. It makes no extra charge of premium to females, railroad
conductors, or police officers.

8. It affords the fullest legal security to MARRIED WOMEN,
WITHOUT ANY LIMITATION OF THE AMOUNT OF PREMIUM they may
pay. By its charter, a WIFE may insure the life of a husband
FOR THE BENEFIT OF HERSELF OR THEIR CHILDREN ; or, a HUSBAND
may insure his own life FOR THE BENEFIT OF HIS WIFE AND CHIL-
DREN ; or CHILDREN may insure the life of a parent, FOR THEIR
OWN BENEFIT ; in each case, FREE FROM ANY LIABILITY TO THE
CREDITORS OR REPRESENTATIVES of the husband or parent. By
this provision, which is *original* with and *peculiar* to this Company, a husband, even if he be *insolvent*, may invest premium for
the benefit of his wife and children, free from liability to creditors.
In all other Companies, so far as we have examined, if it can be
proven that the husband was insolvent when the premiums were
paid by him, the creditors can put in a claim for the amount of
the policy.

PART II.

INSTRUCTIONS TO AGENTS.

APPLICATIONS.

Agents cannot exercise too great care in filling out and completing applications. They should be made as perfect as possible before transmission to the Home Office, not only for the interest of the Company but for the protection of the assured. An important *omission* would necessitate the return of an application to the Agent for correction, thus delaying the completion of the policy and postponing the realization of the commission earned by the Agent. Besides, delays are proverbially dangerous ; and, discouraged by them, parties may in the mean while insure elsewhere. That Agents may not contribute to delays by defects in applications, we invite their attention to the following suggestions :

Be reasonably sure that those from whom you seek to get applications are in *sound health.* Otherwise you may expend a great deal of valuable time fruitlessly.

Applications should be invariably *filled out in ink.*

The name of the party for whose *benefit* the policy is to be made, as well as of the party whose life is insured, should always be *fully stated.* If it is to be for the benefit of a wife, it is not sufficient to write the word " wife," but her full name must be written. So also when for the benefit of children. And as this part of an application is of vital interest to the insurer, inasmuch as by it direction is given to the amount of the Insurance, great pains should be taken by the Agent to ascertain and express the wishes of the insured. Let him distinctly state whether the policy is for the benefit of *himself,* of his *legal heirs and representatives,* of his *wife* alone, of his *wife and children,* of his *wife as trustee of their children,* or of his *children* collectively or individually.

Always state whether the premium is to be paid annually, semi-annually, or quarterly.

In reply to question four of application, as to the *kind of policy* desired, if the premiums are to be paid annually for life, designate the kind of policy by the words "Ordinary Annual Life;" if they are to be paid in ten payments, call it "Ten-Payment Life;" if it be an endowment policy payable at death or in fifteen years, call it "Fifteen Year Endowment," and in like manner of the others of this class; if it be a ten-payment endowment, payable at death or in fifteen years, call it "Fifteen Year Ten-Payment Endowment." So also of all the other kinds, merely changing the term of the insurance.

Compare the replies made by the applicant, as to the "date of birth" and the "age at nearest birthday." If these do not correspond, see that they are made to do so.

Be careful that the applicant replies *unreservedly* to all the questions bearing upon his past or present health. If he has had any disease, let the severity and duration of the attack be briefly but clearly stated, how long since it occurred, whether it has left any bad effects, and if there has been any return. It is the duty of the Agent to see that the applicant makes no *concealment*, whether intentional or unintentional; since the statements made in the application are the basis of the contract contained in the policy.

Let the replies bearing upon the *family history* be as explicit as possible—especially as to the age at death, and the disease resulting in death.

Under the heads of the *health* of the party and his *family* history, get specific replies as to whether he, his parents, his brothers or sisters, have or have not had consumption, rheumatism, or heart-disease, or whether any of them died from either of those complaints. In case the applicant *does not know* the precise disease of which members of his family died, it is indispensable he should be able to state positively that death was *not* caused by any form of consumption, insanity, or heart-disease.

In reply to question twenty-seven, whether an application has been made to another Company, let the person say distinctly, according to the real fact of the case, "Never been refused," or

" Refused by —— Life Insurance Company," adding the reason for refusal, if aware of it.

When the replies of the applicant are all made, suffer as little time as possible to elapse before having the medical examination made. The sooner this can be done, the better for the interests of all concerned.

If the applicant fails to *pass* the medical examination, forward the application to the Home Office, the same as if he had passed; since, among other reasons for so doing, it will afford the Company evidence of the fee paid the Medical Examiner by the Agent. If the party *passes*, fill up the blank recommendation on the left-hand margin of the application with your name and agency.

If an application is made by a husband for the benefit of his wife, he will sign it for his wife, thus : " Eliza Smith per John Smith;" resigning his own name underneath. The signature of the applicant should always be witnessed by the Agent or some other suitable person.

Agents should be sure that the final question (28) of the application, and the declaration and agreement following immediately after it, are read by the applicant before he attaches his signature.

Never take a person to the Medical Examiner to be examined until all the questions in the application have been fully answered and reduced to writing, and the *friend's certificate* obtained. When all the questions have been answered, place it in the hands of the Medical Examiner, that he may familiarize himself with the facts it recites bearing upon the history and condition of the applicant, before examining him.

Never disclose the answers of the Medical Examiner as to the health of an applicant—especially if they be unfavorable. The medical examination is strictly confidential, and should be so regarded by every Agent.

The blank in the application, to be answered by the family physician of the applicant, should always be filled unless waived by the Medical Examiner ; in which case he will indorse across it " Statement of family physician not required." If the statement of the family physician is deemed necessary, it must be procured by the applicant at his own expense.

When an application is fully completed, forward it to the General Agent under whom you are acting ; or to the Home Office, if you derive your appointment as Agent directly from it. It need not be accompanied by a letter of advice; all that is needed as evidence that you think the risk a desirable one being, that you sign your name to the blank recommendation on the left-hand margin of the application.

Agents should bear in mind that, important as success in procuring applications may be, the Company will suffer loss (at least to the extent of the medical fee and policy stamp), and the Agent himself will derive no compensation, if the policy, ultimately, be not taken. It is, therefore, requisite that, before incurring the expense of medical examination, an Agent should have a well-grounded belief in the good faith of an applicant, and be assured of his purpose and ability to pay the premium on his policy when it is presented.

The Company reserves the right to reject an application, even though the risk be recommended by the Agent, and the local Medical Examiner. Such instances will be rare, but when they occur will be for good reasons.

Policies.

Agents should PERSONALLY DELIVER POLICIES and collect the premiums on them, as SOON AS POSSIBLE after they are received from the Home Office. Delay in this often results in a change of views by the applicant. This injunction ought to be promptly attended to, or there will be a large proportion of returned policies, to the mutual loss of the Company and the Agent.

A policy should NEVER BE DELIVERED UNLESS THE PREMIUM IS PAID. When the premium is paid, and not until then, the Agent will countersign the policy in the blank left for that purpose, at the foot of the policy. At the same time he will also affix the revenue stamp accompanying the policy, and cancel it.

No policy is binding upon the Company unless the premium is paid.

If an Agent countersigns and delivers a policy before he has received the premium, he does so at *his own risk*, and will be held accountable for the amount. And any Agent, who *advances* for persons insured, does so upon his own personal and private account.

The revenue stamp necessary to be affixed to the policy will invariably accompany it. This stamp should never be pasted on nor cancelled unless the premium is paid. For all stamps attached to unpaid policies, or destroyed or cancelled in violation of this rule, the Agent will be held chargeable. If the policy is declined, the stamp must be returned with it to this office.

When a policy has remained unpaid more than thirty days after being received by the Agent, it must be returned to the Home Office to be cancelled ; nor should it in any event be delivered if an unfavorable change has taken place in the health of the party in the interval. If the Agent has any doubt on this point he should require the party, at his own expense, to procure the certificate of the Medical Examiner that the party is in sound health.

If, at any time after an application has been forwarded and the policy delivered, the Agent should learn any fact respecting the health, habits, or family history of the applicant which renders the risk more hazardous, he should immediately inform the Company fully on the subject, and retain the policy until instructions are received from the Home Office.

Agents can receive premiums at the time of taking the application, but must not receipt for them in the name of the Company or as its Agent. If a receipt is desired, give your *individual* receipt only, stating that the money paid will be returned if a policy is not granted. If you can possibly collect the premium when you get the application you will preclude the applicant from any change of mind, as well as from the interference of rival Agents.

Agents are not authorized to indorse permits on policies ; to name extra risks of any kind ; to make, alter, or discharge contracts, or to waive forfeitures.

Paid-up Policies.

Agents will remember that by the specific terms of the policies of this Company it is promised and agreed that if an ordinary annual policy is surrendered *while it is in force*, after the payment of three or more annual premiums, a paid-up policy will be issued for the full amount of the premiums paid. Also that, in the case of ten-payment policies, it is promised and agreed that if the policy is surrendered *while it is in force*, after the payment of two or more annual premiums, a paid-up policy will be issued for as many *tenths* of the amount insured as there have been annual premiums paid. Similar agreements are made as to other policies, the premiums on which are payable in a specified number of years.

As these guarantees form one of the special features of this Company by which insurers are protected against the lapse or forfeiture of their policies, Agents are particularly requested to extend every aid in their power to secure their advantages to policy-holders, in case they are unable to continue the payment of their premiums. They will, therefore, observe the following rules :

1. In order to secure a paid-up policy, the original policy must be returned to the Home Office *before* the next annual premium has become due. The policy should be returned through the Agent.

2. It is the desire of this Company that no policy should lapse or become forfeited ; and, if the policy-holder will take the simple precaution above prescribed, his policy need not become lapsed. But in all cases this course must be pursued ; and the Company cannot be held responsible if the policy-holder refuses or neglects to avail himself of the provision intended for his benefit.

3. In all cases where a policy-holder fails to pay the premium on his policy when it is due, the policy becomes void ; and it is then *too late* to apply for a paid-up policy. This rule will be rigidly adhered to.

Premiums and Renewals.

Premiums may be paid annually, semi-annually, or quarterly. In calculating the premiums the following rule will be observed for those which are quarterly or semi-annual: For quarterly, add six per cent. and divide the product by four; for semi-annual, add four per cent. and divide by two.

It is mutually to the interest of the Agent and the Company that premiums should be paid annually, if possible. If they are payable semi-annually the Agent will expend twice, and if quarterly four times the time and trouble that would be required if they were paid annually. Besides, the Agent receives his commissions on the amount of premium actually paid: if the premium be paid quarterly, the commission is cast on one-quarter of the annual premium; if semi-annually, on one-half of the annual premium; and if annually, on the whole amount of the annual premium. It is therefore greatly to the immediate pecuniary advantage of the Agent to make the premiums payable in the largest sum and as seldom as practicable.

Agents are authorized to receive Renewal Premiums which are not past due, but not to give receipts for them in the name of the Company. If a policy-holder tenders payment of a premium of this kind for which no receipt has yet been received, the Agent may give his individual receipt for the money, in which he stipulates that it shall be exchanged for the receipt of the Company when it comes to hand, and that if the Company receipt is not forwarded the money is to be returned.

Renewal receipts will be sent to Agents ten days before they are due; and to be valid they must be signed by the President and Secretary. These receipts must be countersigned by the Agent when he receives the premium, and not before. If any renewal receipts remain unpaid and past due, they must be returned to this office with your monthly account.

If, when the premium is past due and unpaid, the policy becomes forfeited in accordance with its terms, the Company may, as an act of grace and courtesy, renew such policies (but does not pledge itself to do so), upon the assured furnishing to it, at his own expense, satisfactory proof, or the Examining Physician's certificate, showing that he is still a good risk. Upon the receipt of this certificate the Agent will be advised whether the policy is renewed or not, and will be governed accordingly.

The collection of premiums is strictly a *cash* business ; and Agents are prohibited from delivering policies or renewal receipts before the money is paid for them. If they depart from this injunction, they do so at their own risk.

All moneys received by Agents for this Company on account of premiums, etc., are a fiduciary trust in their hands, which they are enjoined not to use for any purposes whatever. They must be faithfully remitted to the Company, after deducting the fees paid the Medical Examiner, postage, exchange (not to exceed one-fourth of one per cent.), and commissions as per contract.

Accounts with Home Office.

Agents' accounts must be rendered monthly, and the balance due the Company be remitted in a draft on New York or post-office order.

On the 25th of each month, and before the 1st of the following month, Agents will make up and forward their account with the Company—as per blanks furnished. They will charge themselves with all premiums and interest collected—giving in detail the number of policy and name of assured, the several amounts of premium paid and date of payment. They will credit themselves with their commissions, postage, exchange (not to exceed one-quarter of one per cent.), and bills of Medical Examiner—the latter to be accompanied by vouchers. The cash balance due the Company must be promptly remitted as above.

No other charges than those above mentioned will be allowed, unless by express permission from the Home Office. When other charges have been authorized, vouchers must always accompany the statement of them.

With the regular monthly account there must be returned to this office all policies in hands of Agents over thirty days, and all unpaid and past due renewal receipts; together with a list of all policies or renewal receipts remaining in their hands and held over for collection.

Permits and Extra Rates.

Permits to travel beyond the limits prescribed in policies must not be granted by Agents, but will be furnished by the Home Office, upon application being made.

Under these permits parties will be allowed, without charge of extra premium, to travel on the ordinary routes of inland travel, by the usual modes of conveyance; and to travel and reside in Europe, New Brunswick, Nova Scotia, and Canada; and to go as passenger between any of the Atlantic ports of the United States and Europe or California.

Permits will be granted by the Company, upon application to the Home Office, to visit any part of the world, without forfeiture of policy, charging only such a moderate extra premium as will cover the extra risk.

Policy-holders who purpose making a sea voyage should always notify the Company of the name of the vessel and her time of sailing, so that we may protect the interests of all concerned by reinsurance, if made necessary by too large an amount being at risk on one vessel.

Females, railroad conductors, and policemen, are insured by this Company without extra charge of premium. Persons pursuing occupations deemed peculiarly hazardous will be charged such extra rates as will cover the extra hazard; but Agents are not authorized to establish extra rates, and must in all cases refer applications for them to the Home Office before making a rate.

Extra rates are always charged as a percentage on the amount insured, and not on the amount of premium.

Medical Examiners.

It is of vital importance that the Medical Examiner be a man of skill in his profession, and of unimpeachable integrity.

In cases where the Company has no local Medical Examiner already appointed, Agents will take pains to select one combining the above requisites, whom they will nominate to the Company.

Blank forms will be furnished Agents, which they will cause the person selected as Medical Examiner to fill out, stating when and where he graduated, how long he has practised, and referring to brother practitioners for his personal and professional standing. Where it is possible, such reference should be to some physician in New York, Philadelphia, Boston, or New Jersey.

The Medical Examiner is entirely independent of the Agent, and no attempt should be made to influence or coerce his judgment by the Agent. Strict attention must be paid to this injunction.

The fee of the Medical Examiner is from one to three dollars, depending upon circumstances; and it must be paid to him by the Agent, whether he recommends the candidate or not. When the fee is paid, the Agent will take a receipt, giving the name of the person examined and the date of the examination. This receipt should be forwarded by the Agent as a voucher, when he renders his monthly statement to this office.

General.

If there is a General Agent of the Company for the State or District in which you reside, from whom you derive your appointment as Agent, all your business with the Company must be transacted through him.

When writing about a policy, always refer to it by its number and the name of the party insured by it.

Agents should never offer to divide their commissions with the persons whom they insure. Such a course would lessen the remuneration and injure the business of other Agents, as well as their own.

Agents must not, in any event, charge a fee for the policy as one of their perquisites. No charge for policy fee is one of the special inducements held out by this Company to persons to insure with it.

Proof of Claim.

In case of the death of an insured person, immediate notice should be given to the Company, whereupon blank forms for the required proofs will be forwarded.

When the policy is for the benefit of a *wife*, the check of the Company payable to *her order* will be issued, and *her* receipt and the policy surrendered is all that is required ; but, when a party insures his life for *his own benefit*, the amount must be collected by an executor or an administrator legally authorized to settle the estate; or, if for the benefit of a minor, by a legally-appointed guardian ; and the *official* certificate of the Probate Judge or Surrogate of the county to that effect must be presented at the office of the Company, with the policy and the receipt of the executor, administrator, or guardian.

www.ingramcontent.com/pod-product-compliance
Lightning Source LLC
Chambersburg PA
CBHW021605270326
41931CB00009B/1374